OBAMA'S CHILDREN

poems

Other Books by Earl Sherman Braggs

A Boy Named Boy, Memoir
Wet Cement Press 2021, Berkeley, CA

Cruising Weather Wind Blue
Anhinga Press 2020, Tallahassee, FL

Hat Dancing Blue with Miss Bessie Smith
Yellow Jacket Press 2019, Tampa, FL

Negro Side of the Moon
C&R Press 2017, Winston-Salem, NC

Ugly Love (Notes from the Negro Side of the Moon)
C&R Press 2016, Winston-Salem, NC

Oliver's Breakfast in America
Eureka Press 2016, Chattanooga, TN

Syntactical Arrangements of a Twisted Wind
Anhinga Press 2014, Tallahassee, FL

Younger Than Neil
Anhinga Press 2009, Tallahassee, FL

In Which Language Do I Keep Silent
Anhinga Press 2006, Tallahassee, FL

Crossing Tecumseh Street
Anhinga Press 2003, Tallahassee, FL

House on Fontanka
Anhinga Press 2000, Tallahassee, FL

Walking Back from Woodstock
Anhinga Press 1997, Tallahassee, FL

Hat Dancer Blue
Anhinga Press 1993, Tallahassee, FL

Hats
Linprint Press 1989, Wilmington, NC

OBAMA'S CHILDREN

poems

EARL S. BRAGGS

MADVILLE
PUBLISHING

LAKE DALLAS, TEXAS

Acknowledgments

Grateful acknowledgment is made to the editors and readers of the following publications in which poems in this collection have appeared:

- *Asheville Poetry Review*: "Still Life" (3rd Place Winner-William Matthews Poetry Prize)
- *Bellevue Literary Review*: "Rainwater, the Color of Ugly Love" (published as "The Color of Rainwater")
- *Immigration Essays*: "Some Call it Gypsy Love" (published as the introduction to a collection of essays by Sybil Baker)
- *The Poet Speaks*: "Sandy Columbine Hook Parkland"

FIRST EDITION

Requests for permission to reprint or reuse material
from this work should be sent to:

Permissions
Madville Publishing
PO Box 358
Lake Dallas, TX 75065

Cover Design: Jacqueline Davis

ISBN: 978-1-948692-72-4 paperback
ISBN: 978-1-948692-73-1 ebook

Library of Congress Control Number: 2021941082

for
Anastasiya Elaine Braggs,
my daughter,
my Obama's child

Walk with me, please,
through
Wars and Small Pieces
of
Love

TABLE OF CONTENTS

STEVE'S SHORT-SLEEVE SHIRT

Steve's short-sleeve shirts were almost always cut-off,
winter plaid,
flannel shirts as if he knew a next winter
might not come.
Back in '71, he grew an ugly afro that
he couldn't figure out how to be proud of, too thin to hold
an afro pick. We were riot-night running buddies,
best friends in the best of times, the worst of times.

We rode the same dull pencil-yellow school bus
during those turbulent school-house years. Our English teacher,
Mrs. Davis, we loved
like young boys love pretty teachers, but
Mrs. Davis wasn't pretty. White as composition notebook
pages, she taught the deconstruction of complex sentences
written in *black* and *white* and *red*.

Unfazed by head rags of race war, she stole our attention,
kept it, never intending to give attention back. We didn't
want it back, anyway. She loved Steve, I loved Steve. We all did.

Steve didn't grow up with us. He moved from the country
to the city our freshman year. Project still-life, still, somewhat,
new. The comprehension of such, I don't think he ever, fully,
wanted to figure out how to measure. Steve was beyond.

Steve was the most honest person I ever knew. One day
during the quiet-riot time of a yesterday or the day
before a yesterday,
Steve and I roamed, randomly, downtown as we so often
did, in and out of stores and shops that had no need
to see us, serve us, give us the time of a weekday. That day

I decided to steal a pocketknife—it was not glued down.
Steve's voice frowned ever so godly upon me, "Put it back."
Putting it back quickly, slowly
I said, "No one's looking, no one saw me." "I saw you,"
Steve said,   "I saw you."

That was to be the last time any of us war-street danced
slow with Steve. The *Wilmington Star-News* knew then
of the killing we could not bring ourselves to believe.

He wasn't on the school bus that Thursday morning
after the Wednesday night fire. Fire truck sirens
were everywhere every night.   Ordinary,
another ordinary day. I wasn't worried, none of us were.

Many school day mornings, we missed one school bus,
then took another school bus. Mostly, we
were never late for school. Mostly, we
were good students. Mostly we
were good government-housing-projects-life kids

during those riot-torn years of city police helicopters feeding
teargas to automobiles
our crying eyes could not afford. Somehow dingy white,
wet towels found a way to disguise us
as young Palestinian war-street boys and the "wetness" saved
us most curfew, moonless nights. But then came
that night that was not so kind to Steve, not so kind to us.

Steve was brilliant, a genius. He knew the answers
to questions before questions were asked, but
he didn't know the mathematics
of his own life,
didn't know how to calculate that that white policeman
knew how cut-off short
his short-sleeved life was "projected" to be. Somehow

2

Steve didn't know the bright bullet light-weight of
a house fire
that night would ignite, without white apology, his shirt,
illuminating so un-beautifully in Negro-ghetto colored
tragic hue,
a weekday Funeral Announcement with his name on it.

Like Magritte, This is not a pipe
Like me, This is not a political love poem

*To all who were
my teacher
and still are*

Don't know if it's a plot or not, but somebody is trying
to kill the art of teaching.
The assassination of education,
attempted womanslaughter, no
crime to speak not of. Love is also the color of love, also,

now, not yet.
Get out a very small piece of paper, a pencil or pen
and write this down.
Somebody is trying to kill the art of teaching. I know
who it is, do you

remember your 11th grade English teacher?
Mine was a not so pretty
preaching-woman when she spoke with the force
of a high wind
from the church of William Shakespeare. No fear,
Miss Irene Davis,
she looked just like an 11th grade English teacher,
when she said, "Come here, let me ask you
a question. Tell me, if you can, why is it that
To be or not to be is a question?"

Fondly, I remember how she'd answer
her own question. Miss Irene Davis, librarian—
cat-eye black eyeglasses sliding down
her pointed English nose,
"Because a question is a question." Zen.

Then, now do you remember fondly
as fondly as I so fondly remember
Mr. Willie Edward McGee, a black man,
and Miss Irene Davis, a white woman,
in black and white photography, backdropped,
framed perfectly
in the dissemination of pure knowledge?

Mr. Willie McGee, he, like a Master Mathematician
masterfully coached as he counted the science of
teaching and learning the weight of paperweight
school children.

He taught 9th grade Every-Thing-Hard-Class.
Counting, Mr. McGee he counted hard and fast
as a baseball curve 'cause
I was a Pittsburgh Pirate back then
when Mr. McGee said,
"Boy, go out there and play center field, see if you can
keep the ball from hitting you in the back of your head."
Said but did not say exactly. But
the way Mr. McGee said
anything sounded exactly like notes of jazz played
between notes of jazz
music, touching me and all of us like Thelonious
Monk touching a piano baseball, hitting home runs
on a trumpet like Dizzy Gillespie to some degree
'cause beyond the pencil-yellow school bus
Mr. McGee drove,
a hurried book of wind drove me and all of us
to school each weekday morning
the Good Lord sent when the Good Lord decided
to come down deep into our neck of the woods.

Somebody is trying to kill the art of teaching
school children the art of thinking beyond
hurried bags of preplanned pipe music.

You know exactly what it is I now talk about, but
let me ask you this, if you may be so kind to entertain
a question. Tell me this.

Way deep down into the darkness of any
dark night,
does a star know how to shine
if there is no schoolteacher there
to measure,
then enhance the brightness in the eyes
of school children?
Take a look at this:
A classroom full of dimly lit lights
begging to be bright. A teacher pacing
beyond a lectern.
The air thick, a thick fog of
fogged-in love. The voices of learning,
loving learning-breeze
ease back the covers of daringly dense fog.

Every student in the room touched.
Every one of them touched by the science of
understanding *something*.
The teacher looks down into the book,
then looks up and into the brightness of
of a classroom full of lights.

Tell me, can you tell by the way a backpack,
a book bag leans up against a desk, a chair
that *learning* a mathematical dance is in the air?
Learning eyes don't know how to lie 'cause,
but, now, do you

now remember *My* Professor, Dr. Denis Robbins?
He called himself a boy,
a Jewish boy from Brooklyn. And he talked exactly
just like that, a Jewish boy. I'll tell you this: That
Jewish boy from Brooklyn made me and each of us
want to come to class
every day.
Every class he proclaimed, whether
he said it or not,
"Don't take my word for it, look out the window
for yourself. Just because I say the sky is blue
does not make the sky blue."

"Aesthetics," he said, "is a going-down ship
in the middle of a black night,
so dark there is no light, in the middle of
a thunderstorm. Thunder angry at itself
for speaking so loudly to nobody but itself,
lightning dancing in the sky like a stage.
You,
standing there on the bow of a sinking boat,
witnessing the bad beauty of bad weather."
Zen, the aesthetics of *learning* to love.

No, he didn't say it exactly like that, but
he did say it exactly like that. Memory
has the right to edit. Still, be it firmly said that
that Jewish boy from Brooklyn
took me and all of us to church every Tuesday
and Thursday from 9:25 to 10:40. Memory

has the right to edit and he edited life as it unfolded
in front of each of us every class that semester.

Somebody is trying to kill the art of
this and that kind of teaching. I know who it is, do you

7

recall the wonder of it all,
your 1st grade schoolteacher, always beautiful
in the way she, always a she, smiled
as she beautifully turned pages, a book.
"Look Jane, see Spot run."
Remember the fun of hearing branches break,
a dog trotting through the woods, cows facing
the camera from a field afar.

Listen now, please, to the smell of a kerosene
lamplight, another stormy night,
a room where dreams are made right up,
right out of nothing, nothing
whatsoever when, then, sudden as not even
suddenly at all, a field of acknowledged
white wonder, a dream of someday
becoming, the dream of a snow day. School-
night children *learning* in the dark.
In the background, stands, always, the teacher.
I don't know if it's a plot
or not, but somebody is killing us, all, softly.

No one has been arrested,
no one has been charged, a blue-collar crime,
a red bandanna loose around the neck, enough
rope, a tree made not of
wisdom and understanding and love, but
a forest fire.

Too many of us smell no smoke, yet, we care, but
still, we choke in fires of silence beneath
a tree of despair. Governments of Disappointment
sent to burn the school house down.

But I played center field
the way Mr. McGee told me to play center field.

I know, we all know
the art of teaching is a smile
while watching flowers and hungry weeds grow.

I don't know if it's a plot or not. But I believe as I see,
the answer I see is always in the question.
And a question mark is not a hard mark to make.
Ninth inning, game on the line, a baseball game.
Play deep, slightly left or right of center,
depending upon the hand of the batter closest
to the front end of the batter's box.
Both sets of eyes,
the eyes of grass and the eyes of dirt
in the batter's box
watching nothing but
the art of being taught the physics of baseball.

Love is also the color of love, also, as of now,
not yet.

What mark, what grade am I going to get
when I turn in this essay late for being late?
I do not know, but

I can hear my darling dear Mrs. Davis,
Mr. McGee and Professor Robbins fondly, probably,
say "Now Earl, this is an A paper, but
I'm going to give you a B because
your syntax is too syntactically arranged,
too loose like a movie, which
I do love, dearly, black and white film noir.
But Earl, you use
too many commas,
too many spliced-up splices,
too many misplaced conjunctions coordinating
too many loose ends, untied without purpose,

too descriptive, your descriptions in
too many places,
too much construction splits, confusing shifts,
too many dangling modifiers
and misplaced modifiers modifying
misplaced words like some misplaced somebody
looking for something
misplaced like misplaced love.

But I do love what you talk about, Earl,
when you talk about love."

Somebody is trying to kill the art of…
I know who it is, do you,

would you walk with me for just a moment longer?
Let's go catch a movie
this Thursday afternoon. The weather is dreary,
a weather-perfect movie set
day. It's raining, but the weather lady has decided
against wearing a raincoat. Let's get soaking wet.
A yellow box office window trimmed in blue neon
ordinary lights.

Popcorn, lots of butter, Coke or Pepsi, some M&M's,
a home-theater red seat, a sticky waxed floor. Dark
like night right before our eyes.
The price of love is cheap, a ticket to see:

To Sir, With Love, a British drama film starring
Sydney Poitier, 1967. The setting,
an old brick-layered high school, shabby, rundown,
London City, England, working class "hood,"
a bunch of bad, mostly white kids,
juvenile delinquents as we call them,
a Negro teacher wearing a Windsor-tied necktie

with a brown English tweed jacket. Handsome,
this American Negro teacher, standing up tall,
standing up tall behind an old oak antique
schoolteacher desk, upon which, scattered
nothing
but a blue roll-call book listing names
next to two yellow pencils.
Floating in the emptiness of clear empty space,
perfectly placed, *The Book of Zen*
which is not visible to the naked eye.

LATE FOR SCHOOL AGAIN TODAY

(a photograph: an Israeli settler protects his daughter during an
attack on the road linking the crossing between…)

On a road crossing the desert pastures of Palestine,
a no-stop-street STOP
sign stops

foot traffic in its tracks, turns
with Holy quiet
anticipation,

faces faces, face to face, so close to the impending
to see what impends,
unbuttons

the top button of a suicide vest and blasts into
oblivion
the slow science of walking to school.

No school bus to ride suicide. My father and I,
we walked this morning into
the evil blue breasts of a vest

disguised by the makeup of a made-up
pretty woman without.
Detonation: fresh green butter

beans blasted into split peas,
still green, between
the East Bank and the West Bank of no

river to speak Holy of.
Market day,
ordinary,

market square fully aware without
being fully aware. Ugly
love in the pretty eyes of an ugly,

cloudy,
maybe-it-won't-rain today.
God must be still asleep.

We keep still, my father and I. Leaf
shaking, without a tree, we, stranded beneath
a vegetable stand table. Overly ripe

avocados implode, guacamole-cilantro.
Onions, diced, sliced
twice like a salad. Carrots, cabbages blasted

into cabbage slaw. Cucumbers, celery,
olives, white grapes, all bleed red. Dead
red potatoes, dead

chicken feather broth,
tomatoes stewed into
dead homemade soup. Harmonic,

a morning menu of an unlucky breakfast.
We keep still.
I can feel fear in the length of

my father's beard, longer than my hair,
my life.
His wife, my mother, a woman my father loved

beyond mistake. Promises, now, so uneven,
so Holy unreal.
The air smells like dead people's smoke.

My watch
chokes to tick. I am late for school.
I can hear bells ringing in my ear.

Here, life is a step-stop stone
in an ancient city of two Gods, one sun
and one moon.

Soon seems not to know how to forget
or forgive. But
how can any God ask anybody

to settle for this life where children fall,
children stay.
Every day we walk to school between

borders and bombs
and stray bullets
with our names already written in roll books.

I am 15 years old,
I am Jewish,
I am a pretty girl without the makeup

my father does not allow. We're settlers,
we've settled into the sounds
of war auditorium music: Mother, dead.

I was 5. Weathered sandpaper
has rounded off the blasted sharp edges of
this, a table we now perch beneath,

clinging to despair disguised as hope,
watching apples trade
stock market prices with oranges.

100% Juice, a tin can rolling down
the sad but shady
side of the road. A bicycle frame with no

front tire can't see its back wheel
still spinning
slower and slower and slower.

Only the children know all too well,
never,
it will stop turning over

the dead face of no promise of peace
on this earth. Blasted
blind, blinded,

a man pats the sacred ground around
his left foot,
looking for his wedding ring

finger. Smiling iceberg lettuce burned
in place.
God-awful smoke music.

Shaking, still, we keep perfectly,
leaning away
from the ills of invented

hate. Late for school, crammed into
the perfect pocket of
a nylon suicide vest. There will be no test

today, no final exit examination,
no answers,
no questions, no nothing but God

forsaken, God awfully bad poetry
blasted into
the blown-up, bulletproof margins of
bulletproof paper.

Marlene Dietrich (A love story)

(trying to remember that movie we watched, but never did finish)

German green bedroom eyes is all I recall. But then again maybe
I am just dream-remembering the placid painted color of green

motel room walls, or perhaps, I now think twice of the overly ripe,
overly over-ready red-green detailed laced box, the mascara made-

up face of an unaccounted-for humid August evening of stark naked
purpose and partly undressed promise. Perhaps, now, I hide behind

the color of red tall ballroom dancing shoes, asked not to be removed.
Red soft silk, tender tights clinging un-wanting-ly. De-decorated lace,

leathery long black gloves that kept sliding down toward me. Eyes,
paralyzed by the hypnotic nature of not enough gin, the deception

of a reflection of two half-moons, full, nippled in waffled syrup, raw
honey circling a heat storm. Burning hot touching tips, lips melting

passionately into the unfaithfulness of our forgiveness as if maybe
tomorrow has nothing else to do but lick sweet flakes of forever out

of carefully crafted exit bullet wounds. The television was playing,
muting out the un-scandalous sounds of exotic pain-spanked pleasure.

We didn't know, we could no longer hear the movie's dialogue. We
only imagined the stage play, *Desire* 1936, only guessed in the dark

what Marlene Dietrich was so taken aback by, so lustfully in love
with, so glamorously, wonderfully enjoying. Choice and chance in that

placid green painted room, that evening, pushed the whole world deep
into the small-ness of cracks between believe and not believe. New Year's

Eve, the rhyme of August nights. So the story goes like this: Some dark
brown handsome, handmade feelings felt the puzzle of white puzzle

pieces and placed, beautifully, each piece perfectly as almost prefect,
exactly where it should not be. Marlene's mirror, back-dropped, pretty,

in placid green, kept looking at us, glued, staring as if Berlin, herself,
was a burning theatre-night room watching the parts we play. Marie

Magdalene Dietrich as Lola Lola in *Blue Angel* 1930 slowly turning
a star-crossed night into a one night, all night, next morning newspaper

stand standing on a street corner without a name, collecting the last
quarters of a movie that kept on playing as we fell so unsoundly asleep.

SUCH IS THE LOVE STORY OF SALLY

(Sarah Hemings, 1773-1835)

They called her yellow children the yellow children
of Monticello. The shadowed yellow sound of lying
noise, yet quiet synonyms reveal such is the story of
Sally Hemings. Even now,

not all, but many, still, can't believe the sleeve of
Thomas Jefferson's pearl button war silk jacket she
sewed in reverence as the never-
intended-to-be-announced Duchess of Monticello.

It was not the first time that Thomas Jefferson asked
her to dance. But first recorded, first in Paris. "May I
have this dance, Sally?"   A quiet question
that was not a question reflected
somewhat clear, somewhat obscure, the ancient symbolic

history of figs ripe in the hazel eyes of a slave girl called
Sally. Sally, his dear dead wife Martha's half-sister.
Sally, his oldest daughter Martha's aunt. Sally, his dear

dead wife's late father's concubine's daughter. Sally,
the child of her sweet song singing mother, Helen.
Sally, the daughter of Virginia dirt and dust and lust.

Proper handles, proper size,
the shape of a plow, in his Garden Book, Jefferson
sketched, yet drew not upon the candor of
previous pages buried   book-shelfed-deep

in the dark, fertile dirt fields of Monticello. Dashing
Miss Sally and their father,

Martha and Polly, the younger daughter, loved
beyond fault, whereas, inasmuch as they could not.

A dangerous decision of the heart, 1789. "May I...?"
Thomas Jefferson's silence   seemed total.
He wrote careful letters to friends and enemies, careful
not to reveal his art of taste
for Sally's dark softness on moon-less Monticello nights.

The politics of a question mark marked in advance,
Thomas Jefferson's life. Drama upon the dramatics of
leaving footprints
without tracks, leaving shoe tracks without the impressions
of having visited Sally's small room at all.

Closed curtain life left wide open. Words of severity,
compulsively controlled. Dream-sung days. Slave-made
shutters of Monticello, propped open on purpose.

John Adams, the second President, tells the story of
Sally's beauty having seen her walking in London city
rain, soaked in Virginia royalty. Sally Hemings, street-
stylish, Parisian clothes, strolling
beneath a pastel pink parasol, listening
to the promenading language of
rain-beaten poetry, listening at a time in American history
that disallowed her black beauty to be beautiful. Still she
was more beautiful than any flower planted at Monticello.

Sally born a slave named Sarah Hemings, 1773,
Charles City County, Virginia Colony. Sally's beauty,
that of a fruit tree. Sally, the shape of   pear-sliced-
beauty sliced
between naked dark honesty and tragedy. Owl eyes

un-flinching, Virginia gentry looked down upon that which

was above their envying whispers,   lamplight love,
the beautiful burning smell of.

Many of them heard, but could not hear Thomas' dear
dead Martha's harpsichord
reshaping the language of red roses and soft blowing breezes.
Between every season there is another name. Pointed words
bruise deep, but love knows not of defeat.   Days of
village voice gentry came to call   upon Sally as a scandal.

To be seen, no elaborate dance of denial graceful enough
to deny the classic story-book beauty of Sally. Jefferson

never discussed that which he did discuss.
Monticello fireplace mantel   silent
as the burning smell of burning wood,
warming the voice of winter weather. Yet

Jefferson never wore a coat warm enough to reveal
the complete dance steps of why Sally's wardrobe
was packed for Paris.   A dusty Virginia

day, 1787. Sally was 14. After 26 months, a French tutor,
Sally returned speaking enough French to unfreeze
the frozen Seine some freezing Paris winter nights.

Big with child, greeted graciously by the dark side of
a slave-shaped crescent moon.   Two days before
Christmas Eve, 1789, the Virginia sun forgot to forget,
forgot to forgive whispering voices of Virginia gentry.

Thunder married the maelstroms of politics, echoing
seamlessly, endlessly across unplowed fields of aristocratic
white folk weeds asking,

"Why have you not married a worthy woman

of your own complexion?" Sally, big with child. They all
knew, but none dare imagine   the resemblance,

striking.   Tom, a baby boy, Sally's first of six
yellow children, white enough to *pass* for white. So they
blended out into the music of far-reaching towns,

taking full unnoticed-public notice of   *passing*
glances and circumstances of. Therefore, thereafter,
they lived a white life
and died as the President's yellow children.

No one knows why as did the breeze not carve
into barks of Monticello trees "Tom Loves Sally." But
whispering winds   singing pine-straw songs

knew the soft steps of   secrets were not secret at all.
They knew, yes, yet none dare say, none dare see
the common consequences of a love story, center stage,

the Camelot of Monticello. A Shakespeare tragedy,
jealousy in the hills of   Virginia gentry. They
called Sally "concubine."
Too beautiful to be or not to be, the tragedy of Sally.

Between every season…. Nothing good comes out of
nothing good. Every direction plotted to dismantle
that which could not be dismantled, Jefferson's love
of listening to lyrics
of reticent rain beat upon the roof over Sally's head.

Chained to the never square corners of circumstance,
Jefferson's silence seemed total, a surveyor's intent.

Time tells, only, the story of a two-term President. Time
tells, only, the story of Meriwether Lewis and Clark

looking for the Pacific side of the State of Louisiana. Yet
time, I guess,
forgot, only, the story of Sally, the 1st Lady of Monticello.

So now with the ease of looking at a beautiful view, look
now, please,
into the eyes of Thomas Jefferson, a Memorial situated
on the Tidal Basin among
flowering Japanese cherry trees still blowing breezes

of slave-made days.   Many dare see the bronze
sculptured, naked nature of forgetting to remember Sally,
sculpted upon marble,
monumental blue. Sally,
sculpted in years of dried red rose petals dried between
the pages of Jefferson's Garden Book. Look,
no, don't look now,
wait, now look.
Focus, no need.
Camera lens of honesty focuses automatically. Any frame
composed
composes beautiful the composition of Sally's song. Snap
a shot, take a picture.
Close shutter speed quick as the speed of no sound at all.

THE ART OF PAINTING POETRY

(When Melissa meets Daud, for everyone, Champagne)

Linseed oil, pastel-colored paint impressionistically etched
into the actual color of unmixed reflected light that night,

the night she met him somewhere beneath the sometimes
stubborn white branches of Russian white birch trees. So

the lack of shimmering leaves remembered their names
as white Russian winters would have them not. Sometimes

the colors of paint forget the words, but the canvas always
plays on, music, like pages of a Boris Pasternak love song.

Van Gogh said yellow is the color of love. Saint Petersburg
was still a yellow city then. Patiently, without words, they

fell in color with the silent love of canvas-covered wet paint.
Real-life and still-life afforded each enough natural light to

see the small softness of harsh rides on subways and Russian
crowded bus stops/steps up, down Nevsky Prospekt (Street).

A song, perhaps the first, they sang on the steps of the Singer
Building, Prince Alexander Nevsky's most notable landmark,

in Soviet times known simply as the House of Books. There,
they read/re-read the short story of each other's eyes. There,

he taught to her the Red Square root of Russia. There, she
taught to him the circumference of an American circle. There,

they taught to each other that color has no shape. Texture
and concept tried to tie her balance to his, still they fell from

atop the tallest roof in that yellow town, spinning, spinning,
down, down at the speed of floating flowers, Van Gogh's

sunflowers, one dozen like roses. A vase, slowly back-dropped
in a pillow of yellow. Soft Flowers land softly, the steps of art.

So there they were, playing paint. Melissa waltzing the way
a red dress waltzes, waltzing across a palette page, a perfect

stage, still-life, *Green*, oil on linen—blown-glass green bottle,
big as the chair upon which it sits—a green silk scarf hangs

from the left side chair back, sweeping, cascading, pleasingly
graceful, elegant. Softly fanning blue, a painted floor. Miles

away in the next room, *Quiet Neighborhood, Venice*, Daud,
slow brushing the colors of slow-drying paint before looking

into the eyes of *Laura in Blue*, (figurative) oil/11.625x7.9375.
Stylistic pluralism, Daud and Melissa, realism and still-life.

The first time they met was not the first time they met, for
they, each, had known forever, the brushing sounds of color.

Repin Institute of Painting painted them before they painted
each other that Saint Petersburg night when the city was still

Van Gogh yellow. I met them in America one art-show night,
a night when the necessary was so unnecessary. Perhaps by

chance, first glance, I knew who the coloring book colored
them to be. Me, I'm a poet. Recognition, not a hard question.

A place of galleried paintings, seemingly miles from anywhere,
a room of art rooms, Linda Woodall's place, a house placed deep,

dark in sacred woods. There in the lobby of painted life, still-life,
my wife and I stood, situated upon edges sharp enough to believe

in the comedy and tragedy of love. This is where we met Melissa
and Daud drifting without drifting amongst tables for tea, coffee,

red and white art-opening-night wine, red caviar and cheese. It
was one of those nights when the moon knew everybody's name.

In conversations banked upon Russian vodka banked upon being
Swedish made, they drove us that evening through Russian city

streets of "The Long and Winding Road." The Beatles took us home as
I remember. Too awake to drive, I was remembering the colors

of them standing upon things remembered. They remembered
blue as the two painters painted Timur, Daud's son, softly into

the picture as the third painter in a family of three. Together,
madly, they all fell in love with what they were already in love

with, the perennially planted brilliancy of soft drying paint. Then
when in Spain, Spain already knew how to spell Melissa's name.

Madrid, ever the kid in Daud's playful mind, knew him as well.
He kissed *Kiss of the Peacock*, oil on canvas. *Delivery Boats*, oil

on gessoed panel, *Evening at the Port, Harbor Conversation*, Daud,
talking on water again. And in Spain where Spanish dirt invited

each of them to plant olive trees and watch them grow, he painted
the matador and the bull. The Spanish sun loved his studio light.

The Spanish moon loved her rhythm, *Spanish Rhythm*, oil on canvas, 76x40cm; *Sevillanas and Stallions*, oil on canvas, 200x100cm. Jazz

in the lobby of a painter's life, a Spanish guitar, a piano. I know paint and colors on canvas don't know perfect. Perfection doesn't

want to know the colors and textures of wet paint. Improvisation knows without knowing, improvisation feels without feeling what

painters and poets and Miles Davis, trumpeting "Sketches of Spain" never learns to name—that which can be named is not the Tao.

Melissa meets Daud, beautiful meets magic, wet paint meets brush for lunch—champagne-chilled, caviar, Canvas Café, and then, Zen.

But What About Love (*The Rabbi's Wife*)

The bottom of what I'm really trying to say, I cannot find,
so if you have just a minute,
I want tell to you how rain falls in love with water. They,

the two of them, never made love. They never intended to,
but what is intent when it's meant to mean what it does not
mean?

They were religiously without question in love
with the sounds of hesitation
in each other's voices. Like rain loves tin roofs, wet as any
water, often
they could be seen like teenagers in love walking
through puddles of rainwater,

together. Him, she saw as particular. Her, he noticed
as peculiar. They
photographed each other, alternately, from vantage points
of mistakes

made on purpose. From the inside, sometimes it's hard to tell
if it's raining
on the outside, but they knew dripping wet is wetter than damp
clothes left, still clinging to clotheslines. She acknowledged
in certain and uncertain terms that she could not be loved
in present tense, so
from the past tense, a page, he stole

and covered it in pencil marks which the rain swiftly washed
away. You see, he was not a poet,
he did not know the true purpose of ink. I think,

neither ever did. Too wet, much too, to care
that Chicago city afternoon.

The moon, most often goes unnoticed
when Daylight Saving Time saves too much
Central Standard Time.

A beekeeper's daughter, she was and he
had kept bees, for years now,
in a box full of inconsistencies and love notes.

A hole in a wall, is it true if it doesn't go all the way through?
Rain in love
with being water wet, yet
she was married, a midnight girl. And I could tell

by the way she carried her purse, too proper to be perfect
like an English fair lady, waiting for the rain
to even out guarded measurements that can

never be cut on a straight line. The Bible, they say, says this
and the Bible, they say, says that.
He wore a ball cap. She, in a straw hat, both too wet to

say anything about what they, both, were afraid to say.
Too cool to care, as far away as Chicago, they were.

I saw it in the color of her eyes. The Bible, they say, says this
and the Bible,

they say, says that,
but noticeably nothing about that Chicago afternoon
color of rainwater.

They, both, knew that in order not to get completely
soaking wet, they, both, had to die a drowning death. So
within the proper configurations of
abbreviated circumstance, the slow dance slowly
crawled

in from beneath and from behind a velvet curtain that was,
for the most part,
already open.
Early, it was, the audience had not yet arrived, yet the stage,
as noted, was already set.

Two chairs, a table, a bottle of red wine,
three wine glasses,
a wall with a stained-glass window left
half-open for the wind of a sincere mistake to blow from.

Behind the scene, the director
was having a drink. Producer and set designer,
already drunk, still drinking.

The Rabbi's wife, her name was not Beulah or Blanche.
South Carolina is a long way from Chicago.
Tennessee Williams said, "Time
is the longest distance between two places," and they
had nothing but.

The rain machine, stage left, hidden from view,
was ready to rain
wedding-night rice down upon
the naked nude pose of the Rabbi's wife
and the principal part to be played,
an unnamed suitor wearing nothing but an untied tuxedo bowtie.

Plot: A map and trying to read directions in a lake-wind-driven downpour.
Musical score: *Once a story like this has been unfolded, it cannot be refolded.*

Some Call It Gypsy Love

(for Sybil and Rowan)

It must've been blue Lightin' Hopkins that stumbled in,
striking them both like lightning in an Asian minefield,

or perhaps it was a late-night late lane change lapse that
just lay there the morning after watching from windows

overcast skies turn into a rainbow. I don't know. R and S
charged and convicted for falling in love with the rapidity

of suitcases. R and S separated by no letters or numbers,
side by side, a line of alphabet consonants. And then Sybil,

not a sound to be made between, yet beautiful in the way
they run together or as if "late for their flight" never did

quite notice that everybody runs away from just as much
as they run toward love. Carry-on bag people, they both

knew that a suitcase is the only case that can comfortably
carry everything. An overhead plane-sized bin says amen

to the randomness of their packing for months in spaces
designed for days. R's mother taught R the safari range

of a rover. S's father taught S to read upside down, letters
after death, revealing a buried treasure of attic-sized words.

R was raised behind a gate of privilege, though he respected
not the bricks. S, raised suburban wild as rural wildflowers.

Virginia American Airline lands smoothly in South Africa.
Baggage Claim claims to understand the lack of turbulence.

Neither grew up in slow-poke city, yet race-car speed is not
the holy essence, timing is their sacred promise. Schemers

and driftwood daydreamer, re-devisors who wakeup-getup
at the break of sunset red to start not the night but daylight

in the way complete semi-darkness celebrates what it cannot
quite see, the quiet sounds of quiet thunderstorms sleeping

quiet under warm blankets of summertime Saturday rain.
On one side of the world, R's father died, buried beautiful

now in stacks of jazz vinyl. The other side, S's mother dares,
still, Virginia in her daughter's daringly keen eyes. Gypsies

are people of no surprise. Kerouac told us that *On the Road*
is a jazzy science. R and S believe in a suitcase god of pace.

It must've been Lightin' Hopkins talking about "Darling,
do you remember me" that they heard that night in Seoul,

Korea. Or maybe Lightin' Boy said, "Take a trip with me"
that night in Seoul, Korea. Nothing but Centerville, big sky,

big eye, Texas blues guitar doing all the sideboard talking
that Van Gogh starry night in Seoul, Korea. It is all there

and here, demilitarized in a zone. We're talking about blue
love, a quiet blue love of boarding passes, updated passport

stamps in blue smoke words, the yellow Latin language of
stage-play-love recited ever so beautifully on the dangerous

balconies and Dover cliffs of life flying nonstop from here
to there. Everywhere stop in Turkey. Istanbul is a bull. So

for now, let us remember cigarette smoke, Napa Valley red
wine talk, a porch perched partially, the shade of a tree while

luggage, itineraries converse weather as two Gypsies part
waters between Johannesburg and Williamsburg, Virginia.

Dancing Around the Idea of Never Falling

(for the spaces in between)

Complete, the unavailing of *Psychology of Misunderstanding*,
Vol. 1 descends again empty from above and spills emptiness

onto a café table, cornered and yellowed by the hollowness
of yellow years and low water marks, marking the highest

point of an impending flood of no tears to be cried crowded
around a sad little table made for two upon which sadly, now,

sits only a salt shaker and a pepper shaker shaking stylishly,
reflecting reflections of each of us sitting across from love. Us,

face to face with the idea of never falling ever again. Love
has a way of sometimes forgetting what we don't talk about

when we don't talk about love. Above the café door, neon,
an exit sign. Menu written on the wall. Everything is *Today's*

Special. Unannounced as of yet, the Catch of the Day. Unsweet
tea by request only. The unexplained cannot explain itself

without or within what has been fashioned to fit. Stop doesn't
always mean quit. Proceed with caution is the color of yellow.

Good farming-weather plaid is my working boy's shirt. You,
 pinstriped-blue, a party girl's dress left over from last night's

reasons not to believe anything we see in a moonless sky. Why
hovering blades of leftover scientific definitions of damage done?

This morning riots have torn holes into the streets of our city.
Looted love, still beautiful, in storefront windows. Mannequins

dressed up now in rags. Blazing bonfires of no explanation have
consumed the silk-covered unmade bed we have now fallen from,

fallen out of like the naivete of playground children swinging
and sliding into the sadness of sad silence disguised as empty

talk. Conversations that know not how to converse convert inches
into miles between us sitting here at this table. Separated only

by the shaking of salt and pepper, I could smile, lie and say
"I love you." You could smile, lie and say "I love you, too." We

both could lie, laugh, look into the voice of our honeyed-eyed,
waffled-face waitress and say, "We're ready to place our order."

SANDY COLUMBINE HOOK PARKLAND

And when one day a field of Colorado blue
columbine flowers wilted into never, what
once was a picture-perfect School Picture Taking Day
angled
flat-out
into the camera lens of something without a name.
Tintype tinted without overtone, no contrast,
too vanished out to photocopy school colors. School
uniforms of dress-coded labels,
we've since been instructed to *Iron Before Washing*.
We don't know why, but
why knows the spelling of each, our names.
Introspection,
time doesn't afford. News-day grief is so brief

these days.
And it should come as no surprise, we are surprised
that we live.
One day after the next, to the milk-shaking voice of
something sour,
we listen to echoes.
Teachers and principals, beyond expended, explaining
what they cannot explain. In plain view, a red fox hides
her cubs in white Colorado snow.
Nights of guarded warnings, too often, forget to fall asleep.
Daylight reminds relentlessness not to re-reveal too much
too soon to us.

It is not safe to say that we would rather not remember
our dreams. We count our blessings by not counting
the spaces between empty chairs. We
ride school buses into the immutable yellow haze of school
morning days.

No front door welcome mat,
no classroom homeroom to speak not of. Love,
2 consonants, 2 vowels, erased
into the relenting rub of a yellow #2 pencil.

Textbooks check out the danger of opening the wrong page.
Library books
check us out as if we know more than they. Hallway lockers,
all, slam sad.
Smiles and hugs and quotes and
"Most likely to…" in last year's yearbooks
tell everything
but the truth
so help us God. We dream in inverted question marks.
The reverse of why is still why.
The reverse of what is still what, but
the reverse of when
doesn't know when to tell us when. 1st period, this morning,
reached down
to grab me,
grabbed instead the frayed seams
of my no-brand-name backpack as if metal detectors
can detect or not, last night,
I completely finished reading *A Midsummer Night's Dream.*

Days in, days out quick as they are slow, we never know
what is which.
Silent,
a red noise circles us
like moving target games at a county fair.
I know you think I should be, but I'm not afraid.
It's something more.
I know you think I should be, but I'm not despaired.
It's something more,
something heavier than the weight of waiting for the other
"something" to drop,

heavier than the gravity of trying to forget the names of
towns and cities
where cross hairs cross out children.

I have never been an A student, I
often question a B,
but I have always turned in my homework on time.

But time, these days, seems no more to care
about homework assignments
to be done at home.
Now-a-days we get full credit for everything, anything
by just showing up the day after the latest network news.
Baby Sister, 14,
and her baby brother,
killed again yesterday in Parkland, Newtown, CT.

A terrible ear it takes to want to hear nothing more than
more gun music.
Arm elementary school teachers some stupid, gun music-
playing politician reportedly said. Dead, can he not see us
walking, almost, already?
Can he not spell his own children's names? Can he not
see, clearly,
what we see?

Little school children, less than 3 ½ feet tall, 1st grade,
first day of school
and every day thereafter standing, pledging allegiance,
point blank, eye to eye, facing an over-loaded handgun
in the teacher's desk,
top right-hand drawer,
left side divider,
next to a roll-call book
that knows the spelling of each, their names.

STILL LIFE

Covid on Canvas, Spring 2020

Six feet deep translated into six feet apart, the complete, sad
design of sad social distance. Every
eye-color gazed to the sanitized floor of a local grocery store.
A spaced-out cross mark tells us to, "Stand Here"   and wait
and watch cans of Lysol disinfectant *scan* themselves as if
the spray, itself, knows we won't go home   without it.

We acrylicize the sad silence of weekdays
when Cleaning Aisle shelves were   stocked full. The next
available self-checkout register,   we wait. Rush hour
is more than an hour. We've learned to sneeze inside out, cough
upside down.   Simple Dawn soap suds, we now worship.
Even "bad" mannerisms, we sanitize through the voices of masks.

No Hugs Allowed haunts even the clothes we wear
these depleted days. One summer that never begins.   We wait.
We have learned the dance
of being too close to forgetting to stay calm, stay stable, stay
at home, work from home, clock-in, clock-out on kitchen-time.
We never knew,
exactly, the number of channels on cable TV, never knew,
exactly, the number of hours in a stay-home day.   But now,
we do.
We've learned to home-school our children,
preschool
to high school by ringing an 8 o'clock am homeroom bell.
Laptops on kitchen tables teach science and mathematics,
ABCs and XYZs

What we've learned,
learns us to Zoom, virtually, from every room.

We, now, calculate the square footage of no empty space
left to paint.
We have learned to open public doors without hands,
greet friends with fist-bumps. We paint disappointments
with calendar squares
of F2F appointment times with better days. Our kids,
we cherish their paint-by-number ways these
be-careful, slow-turning days. We've not flown for months
of airlines afraid to fly. We've lived

for months in towns of restaurants reluctant
to remember to open their family-friendly arms. The bar
next door may never open again. Just yesterday, Starline
Books, the mom-and-pop bookstore where my daughter worked
before college, decided
to close for good and for bad. Packing up boxes of books,
breaking down boxes of already broken hearts, the weight
of these days! Still we rise
just as Maya Angelou told us to do,
again, just before she died.

And as spring 2020 folded, then
faded into early fall school days, *smiling at and to everyone*
we meet as we go on our, now, any-time-of-day walks
has magically,
organically (all natural ingredients) become
the new mental health drug of choice. And
on neighborhood walks, we have learned our neighbors' names,
where they work,
where they're from,
how long they've lived here.
We, now, know more than the styles and colors of the cars
they drive past our homes. And

in this season of street protest for social justice, we have learned
that Black Lives Matter

has never been painted onto the American landscape except
during the prosperous economic times of slavery. We know
the Clorox bleach of hesitation,
isolation cannot wash that stain off our hands. And

in these no-spring-training baseball days of double-play doubt,
days of so many among us striking out,
first pitch, we have carefully
swung for fences of flat, acrylic, interior paint. We've fallen
in love with the small corners between
remembering and forgetting to love. We've been drafted. We're

soldiers in a war of many fronts: global warming, melting job
rates, racial unrest, political up-side-down-ness,
tornado alley expanding, named hurricanes running out of names,
white supremacy rewriting the Civil War,
raging floods, raging Red rhetoric,
raging wildfires
in California. Raging, a pandemic the size of everything
we don't want to know. And

as the world turns to welcome winter, we still wear
the Bermuda Triangle
shorts of summer studio light.
Faith in our front and back pockets next to cell phones
that have deleted the *departed*, six feet deep.   Six feet apart
gait, straight into wherever we walk.   Still life,   we wait
for the full harvest moon of sweet nights remembered.
We have learned to paint the patience of fruit trees.

Rainwater, the Tainted Color of Ugly Love

Burning streets and ugly-news times have undone my eyes again. Now,
at this moment, I hear Nina Simone singing, "I wish I knew what it feels
like to be free." Static African American electricity, Soul music people
without a volume knob to tune in and turn up a nice *life* to live within.
Stationary, the frequency of playing too close to White House flames of
fire   perpetuating   sparks in a nation's eyes watching

the funeral-dead eyes of George Floyd on a dead-hot afternoon in Houston,
Texas, Anywhere.   Answers in America, these days, tend to be framed
as questions without question marks to mark the end from the beginning
of a Black life *that* does not matter: What "police special" color was *that*

police van *that* transported Freddie Gray all the way to his grave, how
old was seventeen-year-old Trayvon Martin when he walked out of *that*
inconvenient-convenient store, why was George Zimmerman's verdict, so
easily, Not Guilty, what was Emmett Till's mother's maiden name? Why

was George Floyd buried in a gold coffin,   why did his pallbearers sway
like church-house jazz, what was that white policeman's badge number,
was he married, did his rhyme and reason rhyme with his "trigger" finger,
how long is 8 minutes and 46 seconds, anyway? 8 minutes and 46 seconds

according to "nothing out of the ordinary" to contemplate is 400-plus years
too long, and America, honestly, wants not to learn to count the arithmetic
of remembering *that* Rosa Parks couldn't breathe, Fannie Lou Hamer
couldn't breathe, Harriet Tubman couldn't breathe, Angela Yvonne Davis
couldn't breathe, Ida B. Wells couldn't breathe, Mary Church Terrell
couldn't breathe. Why? *Brown vs The Board of Education* still can't…

Why? George Floyd, as he lay dying, called out his dead mother's name,
"Mama." George Floyd, 46 years old, Dead On Arrival exactly 46 years,

7 months and 11 days before *that* day.   Obituary: George Perry Floyd Jr.
(Oct. 14, 1973-May 25, 2020), a good son, a loving father, a beloved brother
reduced, now, to the broken neck of a sunflower   mis-watered,
mistreated for 46 years, irrigated in ghetto-garden, dirty,   unthinkable,
Flint, Michigan, weathered rainwater. George Perry Floyd Jr. couldn't
breathe. The ordinariness of *that* ordinary day remembered to forget

it was Daylight Saving Time and that *that* time cannot   not be saved
in the name of George Perry Floyd Jr., DOA.   He called out
his dead mother's name, "Mama," in a weathered voice that rained down
upon the holy drums of Black spirituals, speaking loudly enough to reach
as far back in history as the *Roots*   of every African American family
tree. We...,   me,   I call my dead mother's name every day.
"George, I, too, cannot breathe."   "I can't breathe...,   Mama."

OBAMA'S CHILDREN

(As told by one who rides Nikki Giovanni's Night Winds)

Dear Stationary White Stationery,
I write to you from the point of view of a lightweight
paperweight. I am standing right out here waiting
for you to   EXIT
our local *Zip Store*-gas station so, conveniently, I can
inquire upon you, Sir.

"Excuse me Sir, but Sir, can you spare any spare
change" to spare my Negro-ology-disparity this afternoon?

I use big words, Sir, because I have a small vocabulary.
Inherited habit causes me to refer to you as such, Sir. I
take that you understand, Sir, 'cause

uncelebrated skin-color-coated habit is a hard habit
to break evenly
into the "bad uneven words" I have no choice but
to repeat out here on a begging-daily basis, yes Sir.

In too many *Made in America* ways, people like me
are still, in your mind and in the minds of too many,
cotton patch people, waiting on wagon wheels to roll
us toward indigo farms and tobacco fields aplenty,
sorta like slavery days.
You don't believe me because you believe me, so I'll
say it again like a blues John Lee Hooker love song.
You don't believe me
because
you believe me. Yes sir, you believe me and in me
because
I am the color of wet sandpaper-sunburnt black,
because
I wear my ball cap backward so you can't tell

whether I am coming in or going out. You believe me, Sir, because
I drink only tall cans of Miller Lite, Bud Light, Coors
Light, Natural Light and Old Milwaukee
beer from a Negro brown
boy paper sack every day the Good Lord sends my way.

Jesus and His Mother, Miss Mary, probably won't mind
being my witnesses
when I say to you, Sir, what it is I say: Like Blue magic
parades of marching children,
out of nowhere, out of everywhere they came announcing
the beautiful unannounced-ments of themselves,
Obama's Children.

They look just like regular boys, regular girls next door.
Whether you live in the "hood" as I do or
on top of a red Mercedes Benz hood as you do,
right next door
to you, to me they live. Ordinary, but they are not.

This they, I speak now of, were gifted by a gracefully
laced royal grace, then wrapped like Christmas, carefully,
in the colors of   compassion-colored paper.
I know you don't believe me, now, do you Sir? Listen, Sir,

I know I ain't never been to nobody's college. And to you, I
know without any doubt, I look like I just dropped down
from outer space, a real nigger Neil Armstrong that looks
more like Louis Armstrong blowing into a jazzy trumpet
Beale Street breeze. Please listen to me, Sir. I know I look
like I never read a book, but

I have a GED Ph.D. in the science of Niggernometry-
Biology. I dissect bullshit instead of bull frogs, thus
the high educated cutting guess of gambling words, I use.
The cacophony of   hyperbole, I
use big words because I have a small vocabulary

and besides that's just me and my straight-no-chaser
way of looking at just what I see,
what you refuse to see,
a rosebud bursting into bloom in the spring of rainy years,
Obama's children.

The springtime of America's her-stories reads, reveals
hip-hop kids,
beat-box kids,
backpack kids,
skateboard kids,
computer whiz kids,
Superchildren,
Obama's children.

They are Obama's legacy. You see, they turned 10, 11,
13 and 14
between 2 Novembers exactly 8 years apart. They were
born again in those years "between"
the breezes of
a Maya Angelou song and a Maya Angelou poem.
From the mouth of his wind
of words,
they heard velour-coated verbs, nickel-plated platinum
nouns, sterling silver conjunctions connecting
the adjectives of liquid pure gold that flowed, then paused
stately and heavenly as Venus, herself, disguised as a star.

They heard President Barack Obama's velvet voice calling
forth the favor and flavor of just "Be yourself and practice
within and outside of love."

This Blue Hope Diamond-shaped love, I hear every day
in the way Obama's children smile. I know you don't
believe me, now do you, Sir? Look, I don't blame you.
Blame yourself, Sir, if you need to frame blame. Be sure
to hang it on your nice corner-office
wall so everybody can see it   except you, Sir.

Look at me, wearing brand-new high-top Converse
tennis shoes and a torn-up life. You don't believe.
I don't believe myself 3 quarters of the time, but
3 Thomas Jefferson quarters and 4 Franklin D.
Roosevelt dimes is all I need
to talk you into buying me a cold, cheap can of cheap
Old Milwaukee beer.

Make no mistake, I know I'm not a reliable narrator.
How do I know what I am speaking of? I heard them
college boys talking about reliable narrators
in the assigned short stories they try not to read, so
I know I am not one, I know I am not reliable.
I also know a calculator has no default.
I know, Sir, how you multiply
my bloodshot eyes only to the 1st power. And why is it

that your subtraction of my jazz song is always wrong?
Long division problems in America are too long to divide
when you, Sir,
hide the sums of addition so I can't see the theory
of the string so many of us dark people dangle from
like puppets.   Negro life with a pocketknife
is a Jesse B. Simple life when viewed upside down.
In this city, we live
by the hour. Minutes don't matter
to the shatter and scatter of ricocheted AK bullets.
You don't believe me because you believe in me
and what you perceive as my left-over-from-slavery
red raggedy red ways of pulling empty red wagons
across white fields of cotton aplenty. Any way out is,
precisely, how I got in, how I get into your head, Sir.

So listen up, pull up a Lazy Boy, white lifestyle, white
reclining, white leather chair
and listen to the way
a Negro heart beats when it is not beating.

No, I'm not a poet, not a prophet, I am a promise.

Since the chicken factory shut down, I now work
odd, uneven jobs.
Most weeks I am unemployable 6 days out of 7.
No, truth is I ain't looking for no work no more.
I have been rejected seventeen times too many times,
divided by and into
the way I talk and walk these begging streets. And
that equals exactly what you, Sir, want it to equal.

My knees are sore, I pray, but I ain't been to see
Mr. Jesus in a long time.   Sunday morning
is just the seventh day of a get-drunk week for me.

I know I look like I am, but I am not homeless.
It's just that where I stay is not a nice home
with nice floral-print kitchen curtains letting in
sunlight and reminding me to close them at night.

My life is an open-curtain life, open all the time so
the *Night Winds* can blow in easy as winter weather
looking for cracks
in my curtains of conversation with you, my dear
sad Sir. You
have it made because everything was/is already
Made in America for you, Sir.   Now, take me,

I live two blocks up the street from the University
of Tennessee at Chattanooga. I live damn near next door
to a zoo, an *Animal House* movie,
a frat boy house,
built beautifully amongst "race" ruins of my street.

Fraternity boys, they like me. I love talking to them.
We drink the same kind of cheap beer every night
of the week 'cause weekend nights are just that, another

drinking-stay-up-all-night-frat-boy night. I hear them
through the wall cracks of my boarding house room.

We live (I stay) next to the same railroad track sign.
We listen to the same loud-ass train track noise.
We watch the same parade of made-up Barbie Doll,
partying white girls praying parents don't find out
the real price for missing too many 8 o'clock classes.

We step over the same sidewalk cracks, and when
we are drunk, we stumble
into the same border grass, but they smoke more pot
than I can afford
with the small change I get from you, Sir . "Excuse me…"

I see just about every student in every class
just about every day. Pennies from their tuition fee,
they hand out to me. They are, without knowing, paying
me for the other side of their reality show "real"
public college education.
No textbooks required. Sun Drop-Welfare Science
is a take-home final exam that cannot be graded
by a rubric cube science. Too many holes in the formula,
too many mixed-up colors to align on a one-sided square.

No, I am not a poet, I am a preposition playing out of
position. I don't know my place, never did. I am drunk
as a drunk shrunk on a Wednesday afternoon,
the 15th day of May. I
am just looking, not reading, just looking
like just looking at a book,
seeing those you've forgotten how to see, Sir,
the sunshine faces of super sunlight children,
Obama's children.

I have no hope. They need no hope because
they are hope, our hope. Baptized at birth
in African American Holy River water, they know

not of
night nigger people assigned
as such and such and such as you do, Sir.

They are not afraid of love. They are "Bold as Love"
like Jimi Hendrix playing an upside-down guitar
with his teeth, then pouring kerosene on the flame.
Obama's children have built a new fire in America.

They, quietly, leave blank, on purpose, the race-
space on college and other application forms.
They laugh at you, Sir, redrawing race-war lines,
re-stereotyping a stereo-typical-mindset,
building a Mexico wall, going backwards in time
but not in space. To them, you are, Sir,

a Mr. Day-Light-Saving-Time man, trying to save
a time in American history
that cannot
be saved
in the name of a Religious Right which is,
was wrong
long before race-wall-baseball was invented in 1776.

But do not let the syncopated cadence of my jazz
fool you, Sir. Just you listen a bit more now, you hear.

No, as I have already made un-abundantly unclear,
I am not a poet,
I am poor as a locked door when you can't get in
or out even with a perfectly cut key. Me,
I know you don't trust anything
I say because you don't know how to trust
what I say when I say … Obama's children,

They know without further final examination
or explanation in modern-day political terms.

They know that the 2nd Amendment is not an AK-47
box of hollow-point bullets
and empty shell casings
scattered, blindly, across a school room floor.

Obama's children,
they, too, walked the crowded classroom hallways
out of
and into the front door of
Columbine, Colorado, the front door of
Sandy Hook Elementary School, the front door of
Stoneman Douglas High School. They know, exactly,
what you refuse to know, Sir.

Obama's children, they know
that what you say on a television set, Sir, is not, not,
not, not what Thomas Jefferson meant,
not what Alexander Hamilton meant,
not what James Madison meant,
not what John Hancock's signature signed
up to mean. And they know that you know

that's not what the Founding Fathers
meant when you proclaim what you, so loudly,
proclaim in the name of God. Which God (?)
is a hard question for you to answer isn't it, Sir?

Obama's children,
they are, at this trying, surreal moment
in the United States of American history, a legacy,
years beyond the time they should've been sent.
They know
not without laughter
can race-bigotry be depicted as me and just me
and a bunch of Mexicans America does not want
to keep. According to you, Sir, America only needs
enough Mexicans to pick fruit and mow lawns.

It's a strange kind of strange fruit hanging
from a strange fruit tree. Most of Obama's children
have never
heard the voice of Billie Holiday sing, but they know
the lyric by heart.
They know the un-art of slavery. They know
the four corners of Confederacy is not art at all
as it is purported to be. Me and just me and Mexico
doing our Saturday night ghetto-el barrio no-step
forward dance is all you allow yourself to see, Sir, but

Obama's children,
they know African American History Month
is every moment, every hour, every day,
every week,
every fortnight,
every month of an American calendar year.

Obama's children,
they are not afraid of love.
They are not afraid to acknowledge and celebrate
all that was given to America by the Negro. They
know the real history of Texas and New Mexico.
They know the size of a Native American/Indian
Reservation
Casino
is measured by the weight of Andrew Jackson $20
bills. They know.

Obama's children,
they are Harry Potter people.
They grew up watching and seeing the world
through round, black-brown-rimmed eyeglasses.

Obama's children,
they know the star-shine-light they see at night
is coated by human acid made mistake.
They take no grains of salt for granted. They know.

They grew up riding Day Rave skateboards
at all times of day and night
in forbidden parking lot light.

With no caution to the fall, they all
are the definitions of the surf-board-balance of
wave-walking on blue water.
They cry when it hurts,
they laugh when it's funny.
They still watch cartoons, *Looney Tunes*,
Rugrats, Scooby Doo, Sponge Bob Square Pants.

A rainbow does not know it's a rainbow, but
Obama's children, they know.
Kind laughter, their eyes tell me so, so I know.

But what do I know when all you see, Sir, when
you look at me is me, just me,
an ordinary nigger grown-man-boy standing
outside of a gas station waiting
on an earthquake to make my poverty shake,

rattle and roll up the sleeves of a short-sleeve shirt
that once had long sleeves. Re-skirting the truth
is re-hand-me-down political science book ideology.

Them college boys call me Professor Sandwich 'cause
I love ham and cheese, but Sand Trap's my nickname.
According to Invisible Man in the novel *Invisible Man,*
nicknaming is the deadly art black of escape. This town
only allows me to escape
not from but   into another reason to escape,
if you know what I mean, Sir. You think I look like I
don't know how to read, never read a book, but let me
tell you something, Sir. Jail time is book-reading time.

Some call me Junior boy, but most people call me Sand
Trap 'cause I bogie 18 holes, routine as routine is regular.

My putting 7 iron was born curved the wrong way and
I'm left-handed and dyslexic.   Big advantage when
most days around here are upside down and backwards.

Still I ain't never been able to land a golf ball anywhere
near landing a golf ball on the greens. The fairway
ain't never been fair to me. You know, as they say,
too dark to pay to park in the Mountain City Country
Club Membership parking lot. But,
but nothing. I am
a man in a cage, a baseball (spring training) batting cage,
trying to hit each day
as hard as I can, hoping
for a hole in one
of my socks not to be noticed
by the *Hamilton Co. Coroner's Report* of
a dead nigger
found dead, leaning up against a streetlight, dead-light
post. Backdrop noise, ugly dead remixed music
rolling toward   the end of my credits.

But Obama's children refuse to hear the dead-
talking weight of unfaithful remixed lyrics, refuse
to learn to read the proud, white
sheet music of raining
racism and leftover other 1950s isms like sex

and the extra-ugly weight of baggage, unclaimed,
going and going
around, around and around and, around
conveyor belts called   Baggage Claim
on the ground floor of every airport in America.

Obama's children
carry onto airplane flights the carry-on science of
packing a backpack like packing a small suitcase.
They count their airline ticket blessings without
counting them. No calculator needed.

They fly first class in coach class
because they don't believe in first in class (caste
system science of living in America).

They know Rosa Parks, her first and her last name.
They silently earplug-out noise pollution,
the wailing tunes of 3K air traffic control
discrimination,
anticipation of no landing gear. *no fear* is a T-shirt.
They don't believe in the   "White Myth."
They believe in   Blue Magic.
In ways I can't quite articulate, they seem to believe
as the children of the 60s   believed
in the science of
peace, love, flowers, forgiveness. Obama's children,

they wear overnight panda bear pajama pants
in and on daylight flight patterns. They retro-love
the Rolling Stones, the Beatles, the Who. They
dance to Motown as we did and do. They know
Marvin Gaye and Diana Ross. They know metal
detectors cannot detect
the "rock" or the "roll" or the "soul" of music.

They wear torn-up, winter-plaid flannel
shirts in 4th of July, August heat
not because they're cold but
because they're cool as Colored people cool.

They are not afraid of love. They wear worn-out
Tuesday boots that should have been tossed out
Monday morning, not-to-soon, not because they
can't afford new ones but because
they have learned to afford to listen to lyrics:

Imagine there's no country, it isn't
hard to do, nothing to kill or die for.

Just as the Book of John Winston Lennon sang,
Obama's children sing with the Queen of Soul,
Aretha Franklin's, gospel lyrics:

Gotta find me an angel to fly away with me.

They sing along. An easy, every school day
morning technology children's choir, they are.

They "Lift Every Voice and Sing" like James Weldon
Johnson, sweet-ly, that old Negro gospel spiritual.

In the quiet force of their voices, if we listen, they
teach the teaching of pure ecological examination.

Obama's children, they save the planet by being
the planet. They know, I know, and you know,
Sir, that naturally green-grown organic produce
should not be naturally green
grown organically overpriced to the point of …

They vote mostly blue because they want to breathe
clean air, drink fresh tap water the way we all used to.

But who are they, these beautiful strangers, angels
flying without the notice of wings,   celebrating
the diversity of being diverse,
and why am I standing out here, begging for dimes,
wearing high-top black Converse shoes,
conversing
with a white sheet of white paper, stationary
as ordinary concrete?   Ordinary

just like me, an ordinary out-figured-out "figger"
on an ordinary afternoon,
standing off to the front left-hand side of ordinary,
looking into the eyes of an ordinarily crowded
zip-right-up,

zip-right-in,
zip-right-out, Middle Eastern Muslim-owned
convenient store-gas station, asking ordinary,
everyday, zipped-up-mouth customers if they
have any ordinary,
leftover,
loose pocket change to spare.

"Excuse me Sir, excuse me Ma'am,"
I say in my killingly beautiful, scary, Negro, deep,
muddy Mississippi River, slave-holding state, accented
Southern
charming voice,
"Excuse me, excuse me Sir, excuse me Ma'am, but
do you … would you like to …? Can you
help a brother out this afternoon? Sure is a nice day,
glad it stopped raining.
Thank you Sir, thank you Ma'am, have a blessed day,
God bless you
and you too. Take care now, you hear."

Shark shaking, Southern natured fear of me:
A white businessman
dressed up in a white businessman suit,
handing to me a folded green dollar bill, smiling
a big grin because he's afraid not to smile.

Under my breath, yes, I laugh, I laugh at his cheap,
brown, wingtip, tipping J C Pen-nae shoes, tied up
too tight   to breathe. Patterned leather
for the impending weather, his shoes, a perfect fit.

He's sheet-white clueless. I laugh, but … because
every Black man in America knows that wearing
cheap dressed-for-church shoes
steals all of the expense of
wearing an expensive suit. It's all about the jazz.

You've never liked me, Sir, but you love me
and my musical ways. I know you listen to Coltrane
and Bessie when no one is looking. I know you love
the easy Sunday morning
way I play big band piano notes between brown
pennies, quarters and the thin weight of a dime.

Crime is my first, second and third cousin   removed
(the next of kin) 'cause crime rhymes with time served.
No, I am not a poet,   I am ex-poisonous.
4 years, 2 months, 16 days
in Angola for riding a borrowed bicycle for exercise
on the wrong side of the road is my prison number.

I would love to vote, but a *Felony* on my parole sheet
tells me I no longer possess the mindset to place a bet
on who the next president should be.   So, Sir,

on the second Tuesday in November each election year,
look and you will see me
or someone who looks like me just standing out here
in front of this store, flashing
a stereotypical Negro grin exclaiming, "Excuse me
Sir, but … excuse me Ma'am, but … sure is a nice day."

My tobacco-stained yellow teeth ain't never been
gleaming, Colgate toothpaste white. They have always
been more like Washington DC Watergate white
at night breaking into dreams of breaking out of …

In my never-been-humble opinion, politics ain't nothing
but a white mailbox box full of   white people tricks.
Nigger boy life in a white mailbox
on the side of a rural American road is a love story if
you like love-horror stories told from the voice of
a cardboard box leaning up against
a cold city street on a cold winter night.

Kicked like a football all of my life, I've been.
I have never, not once, been allowed to drift
through the up-rights for extra points scored
on a Friday night,
Saturday afternoon
or on Sunday after church.   The song,

I've always known the National Anthem rigged me
to lose long before kickoff, still
I take my hat off,
place my hand over my heart
and listen to the beating lyrics
of Francis Scott Key every chance I do not get.

I know I look like I don't know the full moon from
a jar full of moonshine, but …
and yet, Obama's children,
they look at me, none of this they see. My face is lined out,
painted in hardness, but they are not afraid of my sadness.

Obama's children, they smell, still, the flowers of
Michelle Obama's White House Rose Garden
where planted compassion of every color grew beautifully
tangled vines, cherry trees, peach tree branches of hope
and acknowledgment.

Without noticing, Obama's boys and girls still notice
a time when time, itself,
acknowledged global warming,
acknowledged the melting of the Arctic caps.

Obama's children, they see you, Sir, smoking
the burned-up coal burning smell of not giving a 3
dime damn about emissions.
They see you not acknowledging Women's Rights,
not acknowledging that Black Lives Matter. And I

acknowledge, Mr. White Piece of White Paper Jr.,
that under your white breathing breath,
you are saying right now, "Why, he makes sense
on paper, but
why is he sitting in the cockpit wearing a sky cap,
don't ya think he's too   dark,
too dumb to fly an airplane?" Let me remind you,
Mr. Blank Piece of White Paper, Sir, that I turn
aircraft carriers around on dimes with the sound
of soul music.
Go home and listen to Sam Cooke cook up a mess
of collard greens, then you'll know what I mean.

It sure is funny how, to you, a small, ragged hole
in the torn plaid short sleeves of my life is a gaping hole
in your United Airline trans-continental sky of
remembering,
understanding,
acknowledging that people, dark as dark blue,
have always lived on American Airport runways. We

have always been your luggage, your excess baggage,
your Negro cargo,
ghetto, "hood,"
you know, American 6 o'clock
News reality show showing up (you)
disguised as catching an alligator
with a police-night-stick-bullet-scattering-nigger-night
special on primetime television.   Revise the re-vision.

Obama's children, they are doing just that, revising.
They remind us all how easily the white myth of forgetting
forgot how beautifully wonderful
Obama's White House years were,
forgot how Barack blue-shape-shifted
red recessed economic sadness into reasons for hope,
forgot how the whole wide world lit up when Barack smiled.

I can see him now, smiling beautifully that beautiful
Presidential smile,
walking like a jazz record recording itself, walking
toward   Marine Helicopter One,
later to be transported to   Air Force One,
later to land, perfectly, between piano and a song.

Barack Obama walked like jazz, talked like jazz. He
showed to white America the Negro,   Black
African American,
Colored people color of swinging   jazz notes.

And to this Colored people color when heard across
this land, the people danced,
some without knowing the steps.
Obama's dance changed how America sees the Negro.

The 6 pm o'clock Nigger News Negro definition of
Black people
all of a sudden
was not the only definition of African Americans.

A Black is Beautiful, Obama's face faced, eye to eye,
the largest white, receptive crowd in American history.
And the dancing people proudly, boldly reveled
in the ambiance of
a Reverence Dr. Martin Luther King-colored sky.

Then one day while the children were dancing
on their father's White House lawn, the sky suddenly
turned dark. November 2016.   Seemingly
the weather people forgot how to predict the death of
a nation. *Birth of a Nation,* un-silently, was born again.

Only in America, the only people who saw it coming
as   Klan-Killing-Kindness-Backlash(s)
were African Americans.
African Americans were not surprised because we know

the size and shape of a lynching tree is white-man-made,
not white-woman-made.

2016 November said to a cold December day, "We
need to rebuild the lynching tree, it can't be Hillary."

No, I am not a poet, not a prophet, but a promise.
I am what I am,
a Negro with thick lips and a wide-open nose. I know,
exactly, the combed-over smell of   racism.
Hurried yellow wooden hair burning   smells,
exactly,   as it has always smelled.
You don't believe me because you believe me, Sir.

The white myth of forgetting forgot, on purpose,
to remember the   pure purple-ness of poetry.
Maya Angelou, wrapped in the newborn smell of
Obama's baby blanket and Obama's baby shoes, told
the nation,   The United States of America,
"When hope is dead,   *Still I Rise.*"
African Americans were not surprised that November,
Wednesday (the day after) morning.

Every African American knows
why my shoes are untied on purpose,
knows why my beard is untrimmed on purpose,
knows why I wear my ball cap backward on purpose,
knows, exactly, why

a lot of them rich white college boys love talking to me
as if 2 quarters and a dime held tightly together slide so
easily into the dark nigger nature of a vending machine.

As I told you, I see just about every student just about
every day, but almost never do I see a black professor
strolling proudly across campus carrying a satchel full of
college knowledge.

Maybe that's why some of them white college boys
call me *professor* as a joke they are not joking about.

Maybe they need me.
Maybe them rich white boys need me,
maybe, more than I need the thin weight of pocket change,
quarters, nickels, pennies and dimes. Maybe

I'll stop talking and tell you, exactly, what I was just about
to say about that day
the Reverence Dr. Martin Luther King Jr. clear blue sky
dropped,
the day the music stopped, and we stopped dancing, but
I won't. What I will tell you is this:

Obama's children kept dancing. They are still dancing
to an orchestra of love lyrics, unprintable
in black and white
pencil marks that mark a new day in America's history.

Soundwaves travel forever and forever young
are the young ears pierced by Obama's words
of compassion and acceptance. They are not afraid of
love, and love is not afraid of them.

Take me for an example, Sir, if you need an example.
I dropped out of high school
before I dropped out of high school.
You know my story
well, Sir, better than most. But somehow, I learned
to write insidiously   sharp, cutting words,
pretty as a poet,
words that remind me that I talk too much.

So let me and it suffice to say, they, Obama's children
come quiet as an army of answers   not questions.

They come wearing coats, jackets and hats of
pure understanding and forgiveness.
Their biological parents never once had to tell them
to honor our differences.
The President of the United States of America told them
and they listened.
They grew up riding skateboards, perfecting the ever elusive
science of balance, walking   on water.
Race and gender equality is as natural for them
as a cool drink of spring bottled water
on a hot hiking-up-a-mountain day. They grew up   royal
as Windsor Castle in a White House designed and decorated
by their African American,
Black,
Negro
Colored parents, Mr. and Mrs. Barack and Michelle Obama.
They grew up side by side with their sisters, Sasha and Malia.
They grew up listening to, learning from and   loving
Michelle's mother, their grandmother   Marian Robinson.

Their biological parents never had to tell them, "When
you grow up, you can be anything   you want to be."
The first Black President of the United States of America
showed them,
told them and they listened without ever knowing they
were   listening to what they were hearing:
The wonderful blooming and blossoming sounds flower
gardens make when flowers are watered long, deep, slow.

They learned early that the effects of an easy answer
is the easiest way to break a heart. They don't believe
as you believe, Sir.   Like so many, you
think that you can drink a bottle of poison and not die.
Why?
They don't ask us why, they tell us why, don't ask us how,
they show us how to love the blue color of blue magic.
They listen to the music of   love
in the voices of Lorde, 21 Pilots and Neon Trees. They

believe trees can be saved. They dismiss the stage play
of bigotry by not buying a ticket.
They know the melting pot
has been melting too long to not have melted yet.
They travel in groups diverse as the universe.
They count lucky stars without counting them.
They know without knowing that they know
Obama's last standing ovation is still standing.

The cadence of Obama's velvet voice still calls forth
his children. From every part of this country, they ride
skateboards,   balanced upon the center of
things   too many of us are afraid to acknowledge.

They know the chemical reaction to love is love. And

I love President Barack Obama. To me, he will always
be the quintessential   American Statesman.

I use big words because I have a small vocabulary. You
use big words to impress. But Sir, may I remind you,
that *Impressionism* paints, and paintings are wordless.
Sincerely, yours truly,
Mr. Samuel S. Trap
PS,
FYI
and just so you know: The American weather forecast,
from now on, will be predicted
by a diversity of pregnant weather women
giving birth to Obama children's children. I know
you now know
you don't believe me, Sir, because you believe me, Sir.
Amen
I'll say it again like a blues John Lee Hooker love song.
Amen

ABOUT THE AUTHOR

A country boy from Wilmington N.C., **Earl S. Braggs** is a UC and Battle Professor of English at the U of Tennessee at Chattanooga. His awards include the International Jack Kerouac Literary Prize and the Anhinga Poetry Prize. Braggs is the author of fourteen poetry collections, including *Negro Side of the Moon* and *Ugly Love*.